Buckle
Shoe

To renew or order library books visit
www.lincolnshire.gov.uk
You will require a Personal Identification Number.
Ask any member of staff for this

One, two, buckle my shoe ;

£4.99   J398.8   JNF

L 5/9

Copyright © QED Publishing 2004

First published in the UK in 2004 by
QED Publishing
A Quarto Group Company
226 City Road
London, EC1V 2TT

www.qed-publishing.co.uk

A Catalogue record for this book is available from the British Library.

ISBN 1 84538 309 5

Compiled by Anne Faundez
Designed by Alix Wood
Editor Hannah Ray
Illustrated by Brett Hudson

Series Consultant Anne Faundez
Creative Director Louise Morley
Editorial Manager Jean Coppendale

Printed and bound in China

Start Reading
AND TALKING

One, Two, Buckle My Shoe

Compiled by Anne Faundez

QED Publishing

Hickory dickory dock,
The mouse ran up the clock.
　　The clock struck one,
　　The mouse ran down,
Hickory dickory dock.

Incy Wincy spider
Climbed up the water spout.
Down came the rain
And washed poor spider out.
Out came the sun
And dried up all the rain,
Incy Wincy spider
Climbed up the spout again.

Higgledy, piggledy, pop!
The dog has eaten the mop;
The pig's in a hurry,
The cat's in a flurry,
Higgledy, piggledy, pop!

Oh, the grand old Duke of York,
He had ten thousand men,
He marched them up to the top of the hill,
And he marched them down again.

And when they were up, they were up,
And when they were down, they were down,
And when they were only half way up,
They were neither up nor down.

If you're happy and you know it,
Clap your hands;
If you're happy and you know it,
Clap your hands;
If you're happy and you know it
And you really want to show it,
If you're happy and you know it
Clap your hands.

If you're happy and you know it,
Stamp your feet;
If you're happy and you know it,
Stamp your feet;
If you're happy and you know it
And you really want to show it,
If you're happy and you know it
Stamp your feet.

I'm a little teapot, short and stout,
Here's my handle, here's my spout.
When I see the teacups, hear me shout,
Tip me up and pour me out!

Mary, Mary, quite contrary,
How does your garden grow?
With silver bells and cockleshells,
And pretty maids all in a row.

Hey, diddle, diddle,
The cat and the fiddle,
The cow jumped over the moon.
The little dog laughed
To see such sport,
And the dish ran away with
    the spoon.

Humpty Dumpty sat on a wall,
Humpty Dumpty had a great fall.
All the king's horses and all the king's men
Couldn't put Humpty together again.

Old MacDonald had a farm,
E-I-E-I-O!

And on that farm he had some pigs,
E-I-E-I-O!

With an oink oink here
and an oink oink there
here an oink
there an oink
everywhere an oink, oink!

Old MacDonald had a farm,
E-I-E-I-O!

And on that farm he had some ducks,
E-I-E-I-O!

With a quack quack here
and a quack quack there
here a quack
there a quack
everywhere a quack, quack!

Old MacDonald had a farm,
E-I-E-I-O!

I had a little nut tree
And nothing would it bear
But a silver nutmeg and a golden pear.

The King of Spain's daughter came to visit me,
And all for the sake of my little nut tree.

I skipped over water, I danced over sea,
And all the birds in the air couldn't catch me.

The Queen of Hearts
She made some tarts,
All on a summer's day.
The Knave of Hearts
He stole those tarts,
And took them clean away.

Old Mother Hubbard
Went to the cupboard,
To fetch her poor dog a bone;
    But when she got there,
    The cupboard was bare
And so the poor dog had none.

She went to the fruiterer's
    To buy him some fruit;
But when she came back,
    He was playing the flute.

She went to the hatter's
To buy him a hat;
But when she came back,
He was feeding the cat

The dame made a curtsy,
The dog made a bow,
The dame said, "Your servant."
The dog said, "Bow-wow."

19

One, two, buckle my shoe
Three, four, knock at the door
Five, six, pick up sticks
Seven, eight, lay them straight
Nine, ten,
A big fat hen!

HEN 1

Twinkle, twinkle little star,
How I wonder what you are.
Up above the world so high
Like a diamond in the sky.
Twinkle, twinkle little star,
How I wonder what you are.

What do you think?

Humpty Dumpty
What did Humpty
Dumpty fall off?

**Higgledy,
Piggledy, Pop!**
What has the
dog eaten?

Hey, Diddle, Diddle

Can you remember who jumped over the moon?

The Queen of Hearts

Who stole the Queen of Heart's tarts?

Carers' and teachers' notes

- Choose a nursery rhyme to read to your child, and then invite him/her to join in as you re-read it.
- Together, act out the rhyme 'Incy Wincy spider'. Encourage your child to take on the role of Incy climbing up the water spout, while you act out the sun (smiling face) and the rain (hands fluttering downwards).
- Together, invent actions for the poem 'Higgledy, Piggledy, Pop!'.
- Act out the rhyme 'If You're Happy and You Know It' by clapping hands and stamping feet at appropriate times.
- Together, recite and march to the rhythm of 'The Grand Old Duke of York'.
- While you read 'Old MacDonald had a Farm', ask your child to act out the animal choruses, making the noises for 'oink, oink!' and 'quack, quack!'.

- Ask your child if he/she can think of another animal that Old MacDonald might have on his farm. What noise does the animal make? Add a verse to the original rhyme, about this animal.
- Sing the tune for 'I Had a Little Nut Tree'. If you are not familiar with the tune, create one together.
- 'Mary, Mary, Quite Contrary' is for two voices. Decide which of you will ask the question, and which of you will reply as Mary. Read the rhyme again, helping your child with his/her part.
- Ask your child which is his/her favourite nursery or action rhyme. Why does he/she like this poem?
- Can your child learn by heart his/her favourite rhyme and act it out for you?
- Ask your child to draw and colour a scene from his/her favourite rhyme.